TRANSFORMING

# GRACE

## LIVING CONFIDENTLY IN GOD'S UNFAILING LOVE

**A DISCUSSION GUIDE BASED ON THE BOOK**

# JERRY BRIDGES

NAVPRESS ●™
A MINISTRY OF THE NAVIGATORS
P.O. BOX 35001, COLORADO SPRINGS, COLORADO 80935

## Our Guarantee to You

We believe so strongly in the message of our books that we are making this quality guarantee to you. If for any reason you are disappointed with the content of this book, return the title page to us with your name and address and we will refund to you the list price of the book. To help us serve you better, please briefly describe why you were disappointed. Mail your refund request to: NavPress, P.O. Box 35002, Colorado Springs, CO 80935.

The Navigators is an international Christian organization. Our mission is to reach, disciple, and equip people to know Christ and to make Him known through successive generations. We envision multitudes of diverse people in the United States and every other nation who have a passionate love for Christ, live a lifestyle of sharing Christ's love, and multiply spiritual laborers among those without Christ.

NavPress is the publishing ministry of The Navigators. NavPress publications help believers learn biblical truth and apply what they learn to their lives and ministries. Our mission is to stimulate spiritual formation among our readers.

ISBN 08910-96442

Unless otherwise identified, all Scripture in this publication is taken from the *Holy Bible: New International Version* (NIV®). Copyright © 1973, 1978, 1984 by International Bible Society. Used by permission of Zondervan Bible Publishers. Another version used is *The New Testament in Modern English* (PH), J.B. Phillips Translator, © J.B. Phillips 1958, 1960, 1972, used by permission of Macmillan Publishing Company.

Printed in the United States of America

9 10 11 12 13 14 15 16 17 18 / 05 04 03 02 01 00

# CONTENTS

# AUTHOR

Jerry Bridges, formerly Vice President for Corporate Affairs of The Navigators, is a staff member with The Navigators' Community Ministries Group, where he is engaged primarily in a Bible teaching ministry.

He grew up in Tyler, Texas, and is a graduate of the University of Oklahoma. While serving as an officer in the United States Navy, Jerry came in contact with The Navigators and soon felt God's call on his life to that ministry. He has served The Navigators' staff since 1955.

Jerry is also the author of *The Pursuit of Holiness*, *The Practice of Godliness*, *Trusting God*, and *The Discipline of Grace*.

Jerry and his wife, Jane, live in Colorado Springs.

5

# INTRODUCTION

Grace. It truly is amazing. But why do so few Christians *experience* the joy of knowing God and His infinite grace? Since it is by God's grace that we are saved, and by His grace that we grow, what is our part in this process? In this study you will explore these and other questions about grace. In the end, hopefully you will come away with a deeper understanding and a fuller experience of the amazing grace of our Lord.

This study guide is for use with the book *Transforming Grace* (NavPress, 1991), but it can also be used by itself. Each lesson contains a short excerpt from that book. Also, while this study guide is written to stimulate group discussions, you can use it for individual study. The section at the back of the book called "Help for Leaders" gives practical suggestions about how to lead a group through this study.

Each lesson contains the following sections:

*Central Idea.* This states the main point of the lesson. It will be helpful to keep this in mind while you prepare the lesson and during group discussions.

*Warm-up.* This ice-breaker question will help the group warm up at the beginning of the sessions, and introduce the topic of discussion.

*Text.* This material is taken from the book *Transforming Grace.* Group members should read this portion before getting together.

*Exploring Grace.* These questions help you grapple with the ideas in the text as you look at relevant Scripture passages. They will challenge you to think about how these truths relate to your particular circumstances.

*Closing Prayer.* These suggestions are designed to help your closing prayer time relate to the lesson. Also, at this time the group should intercede for personal needs people shared during the discussion.

*Going Deeper.* These are extra questions for additional study and discussion if time allows. The leader can draw from these questions if more material is needed.

*Pondering Grace.* These quotes are for personal reflection and for stimulating further thought. They may also help broaden the discussions.

God's grace is not something abstract and theoretical in the life of faith. It is the essential and pervasive means by which God impacts our lives. To know God's grace is to see His hand at work transforming our lives. May His grace draw you deeper into fellowship with Him.

# THE PERFORMANCE TREADMILL

## CENTRAL IDEA

**God's grace alone saves us, helps us grow, meets our daily needs, and guarantees our future in heaven. These blessings are never given to us based on our performance.**

## WARM-UP

Tell about a time when someone (a parent, teacher, or friend) treated you with grace instead of treating you as your behavior deserved.

## THE PERFORMANCE TREADMILL

❝ One of the best kept secrets among Christians today is this: Jesus paid it all. I mean all. *He not only purchased your forgiveness of sins and your ticket to Heaven, He purchased every blessing and every answer to prayer you will ever receive.* Every one of them—no exceptions.

Why is this such a well-kept secret? For one thing we are afraid of this truth. We are afraid to tell even ourselves that we don't have to work anymore, that the work is all done. We are afraid that if we really believe this, we will slack off in our Christian duties. Having come into God's Kingdom by grace alone solely on the merit of Another, we're now trying to pay our own way by our performance. We try to live by good works rather than by grace.

The Christian's debt has been paid by the death of Christ. The law of God and the justice of God have been fully satisfied. The debt of our sins has been marked "Paid in Full!" God is satisfied and so are we. We have peace with God, and we are delivered from a guilty conscience (Romans 5:1, Hebrews 10:22).

We are brought into God's Kingdom by grace; we are sanctified (the process of growing in our faith to become more like Christ) by grace; we receive both temporal and spiritual blessings by grace; we are motivated to obedience by grace; we are called to serve and enabled to serve by grace; we receive strength to endure trials by grace; and finally, we are glorified by grace. The entire Christian life is lived under the reign of God's grace.

What, then, is the grace by which we are saved and under which we live? *Grace* is God's free and unmerited favor shown to guilty sinners who deserve only judgment. It is the love of God shown to the unlovely. It is God reaching downward to people who are in rebellion against Him.

And although this is a study about *living* by grace, we need to be sure we first understand *saving* grace. Everything that I say about the grace of God in subsequent lessons assumes that you have experienced the *saving* grace of God—that you have trusted in Jesus Christ alone for eternal salvation. I would do you a fatal injustice if I allowed you to believe that all the wonderful provisions of God's grace we will see in the following lessons are yours apart from salvation through Jesus Christ.

I once heard a definition of grace as God's making up the difference between the requirements of His righteous law and what we lack in meeting those requirements. No one is good enough to earn salvation by himself, this definition said, but God's grace simply makes up what we lack.

To say the grace of God makes up the difference of what God requires of us is like comparing two people's attempts to leap across the Grand Canyon. The canyon averages about nine miles in width from rim to rim. Suppose one person could leap out about thirty feet while another can leap only

10

six feet. What difference does it make? Sure, one person can leap five times as far as the other, but relative to nine miles (47,520 feet!), it makes no difference. When God built a bridge across the "Grand Canyon" of our sin, He didn't stop thirty feet or even six feet from our side. He built the bridge all the way.

The Bible never speaks of God's grace as simply making up our deficiencies—as if salvation consists in so much good works (even a variable amount of good works) plus so much of God's grace.

All of us, the saint as well as the sinner, need God's grace. The most conscientious, dutiful, hardworking Christian needs God's grace as well as the most dissolute, hard-living sinner. All of us need the same grace. The sinner does not need more grace than the saint, nor does the immature believer need more than the missionary. We all need the same amount of grace because the "currency" of our good works is debased and worthless before God.

Here is a spiritual principle regarding the grace of God: *To the extent you are clinging to any vestiges of self-righteousness or are putting any confidence in your own spiritual attainments, to that degree you are not living by the grace of God in your life.* This principle applies both in salvation and in living the Christian life. Grace and good works (that is, works done to earn favor with God) are mutually exclusive. We cannot stand, as it were, with one foot on grace and the other on our own works of merit.

If you are trusting to *any* degree in your own morality or religious attainments, or if you believe that God will somehow recognize any of your good works as merit toward your salvation, you need to seriously consider if you are truly a Christian. I realize I risk offending some with that statement, but we must be absolutely clear about the truth of the gospel of salvation. (Taken from chapters 1 and 2 of *Transforming Grace*.) 🙶

### EXPLORING GRACE

1. a. What do the following verses say about your spiritual condition apart from Christ?

Isaiah 53:6


Romans 3:10-20


b. Relate an experience that made you keenly aware of
your spiritual "bankruptcy" apart from Christ.


2. Why is it important to focus on your spiritual condition
apart from Christ in order to understand God's grace?


3. In Philippians 3:1-14 Paul contrasts the attitude of
legalism with a true understanding of the transforming
grace of God. In the following chart, contrast a legalist
trying to earn God's favor and a person trusting in
God's grace.

|  | Legalist | One Trusting in Grace |
|---|---|---|
| Basis of a relationship with God | | |
| Feelings toward God | | |
| Motivation for good behavior | | |
| Reasons for feeling bad about failures | | |
| Treatment of others who have fallen short | | |
| Basis of strength during trials | | |
| Basis of strength to serve the Lord | | |

4. Many Christians believe that their justification is based on grace, the blessings in their Christian life are based on works, and their future glorification will be based on grace. Where is the error in this thinking? (See Galatians 3:3 and Philippians 1:6.)

5. Look at the following verses. What do they teach about trying to mix grace and works as the basis for a relationship with God?

Romans 11:6

Galatians 5:2-6

6. What do you think makes it so hard for a person to rely on God's grace rather than his own efforts?

7. Give an example of a recent time when you were tempted to think that God's blessings in your life depended on your performance. For example:

◆ You missed your quiet time. When things went wrong during the day, you attributed it to God's disappointment with you for missing your time with Him.

◆ You had an especially worshipful time with the Lord, reading His word, praising Him, and interceding for your friends. When you needed the Lord's help with a particular problem, you felt He owed you this favor.

8. Do you ever experience feelings of self-righteousness and spiritual pride creeping into your life? In what circumstances do you find yourself most vulnerable to these kinds of thoughts?

9. How can you guard against these attitudes of self-righteousness and spiritual pride? Decide on one specific thing you plan to do this week to guard against depending on your performance to earn God's favor. For example:

   a. For one day, keep a running tally on a three-by-five-inch card of the times you think sinful thoughts. Each time you make a mark on the card, stop and thank God that your forgiveness was procured at Calvary, and that by His grace you are growing in Him.

   b. Make a list of God's blessings in your life in the last year. Put a check beside anything on your list that you earned through your behavior.

c. Make a list of some of your accomplishments in life. Put a check beside any that you achieved on your own efforts, without *any* help from God.

## CLOSING PRAYER

At this time, pray for any personal needs mentioned during the discussion. Praying for one another's needs will bind your group closer together. Spend some of your prayer time thanking God for His boundless grace in your lives.

GOING DEEPER (Extra questions for further study)

1. What insights do the following verses give us about God's view of our sin?

   Leviticus 16:1-34

   2 Samuel 12:9-10

   1 Kings 13:21-22

2. Sometimes the word *sin* doesn't mean anything to a non-believer. How would you explain the concept of sin without using the word? (You might want to look up the word *sin* in a Bible dictionary or a thesaurus.)

3. What is the relationship between the grace of God and the righteousness of Christ?

   Romans 3:22-24

   Galatians 5:2-4

   Ephesians 2:4-7

4. Which person needs God's grace more: the conscientious, dutiful, hardworking Christian, or the most decadent, hard-living sinner? Explain your answer.

## PONDERING GRACE (For personal reflection)

*The first and possibly most fundamental characteristic of divine grace is that it presupposes sin and guilt. Grace has meaning only when men are seen as fallen, unworthy of salvation, and liable to eternal wrath. . . . Grace does not contemplate sinners merely as undeserving but as ill-deserving. . . . It is not simply that we do not deserve grace; we* do *deserve hell.*

C. Samuel Storms, *The Grandeur of God*

*Let grace be the beginning, grace the consummation, grace the crown.*

Bede

*Grace is love that cares and stoops and rescues.*

John R. W. Stott

*Grace ceases to be grace if God is compelled to bestow it in the presence of human merit. Grace ceases to be grace if God is compelled to withdraw it in the presence of human demerit. Grace is treating a person without the slightest reference to desert whatsoever, but solely according to the infinite goodness and sovereign purpose of God.*

C. Samuel Storms, *The Grandeur of God*

*Divine grace disdains to be assisted in the performance of that work which peculiarly belongs to itself, by the poor, imperfect performances of men. Attempts to complete what grace begins, betray our pride and offend the Lord; but cannot promote our spiritual interest. Let the reader therefore, carefully remember, that grace is either absolutely free, or it is not at all: and, that he who professes to look for salvation by grace, either believes in his heart to be saved entirely by it, or he acts inconsistently in affairs of the greatest importance.*

Abraham Booth, *The Reign of Grace*

LESSON TWO

# GRACE—
# IT REALLY IS AMAZING

## CENTRAL IDEA

**In His infinite grace, God does not treat us as we deserve, but rather offers us forgiveness through faith in Christ. Christ removes our guilt and puts in its place His righteousness. The blessings we receive come to us through faith in Jesus Christ, not because of anything we have done.**

## WARM-UP

Imagine for a moment that next time you pray you will have to come into God's presence based on your own merit. What things would you be able to say you have accomplished? Do they outweigh the times you have failed God? Now, give each person a chance to answer this question: "How does trying to come into God's presence on your own merits make you feel?"

## GRACE—IT REALLY IS AMAZING

**66** A study of the grace of God is a study in contrast, a contrast between the desperate plight of mankind and the abundant and gracious remedy God has provided for us through Christ Jesus.

Because of God's grace we are declared righteous before Him. We are all guilty before God—condemned, vile, and

19

helpless. We had no claim on God; the disposition of our case was wholly up to Him. He could with total justice have pronounced us all guilty—for that is what we were—and consigned us all to eternal damnation. He owed us nothing; we owed Him everything.

In Ephesians 2:1-9 we see the contrast drawn so sharply between our ruin and God's remedy. We were dead in our transgressions, but God intervened. We were in bondage to sin, but God intervened. We were objects of wrath, but God intervened. God, who is rich in mercy, intervened. Because of His great love for us, God intervened and made us alive with Christ, even when we were dead in our transgressions and sins. All this is summed up in one succinct statement, "It is by grace you have been saved" (Ephesians 2:8). Our condition was hopeless, but God intervened in grace.

God's grace, then, does not supplement our good works. Instead, God's grace overcomes our *bad* works, which are our sins. God did this by placing our sins on Christ and by letting fall on Him the wrath we so richly deserved. Because Jesus completely paid the awful penalty of our sins, God could extend His grace to us through complete and total forgiveness of our sins.

If you have trusted Christ as your Savior, then all the expressions of God's forgiveness given to us throughout Scripture are true for you. He has removed your sins as far as the east is from the west (Psalm 103:12). He has put them behind His back and hurled them into the depths of the sea (Isaiah 38:17, Micah 7:19). He has blotted them out of His record book and promised never to bring them up again (Isaiah 43:25). You are free from accusation—not because of anything whatsoever in you, but because of His grace alone through Jesus Christ (Colossians 1:21-22).

Are you willing to believe this wonderful truth and live by it? You may reply, "I do believe it. I do believe my sins are forgiven and I will go to Heaven when I die." But are you willing to *live* by it today, in this life? Will you accept that God not only *saves* you by His grace through Christ but also *deals* with you day by day also by His grace?

Why then do we not experience more of this endless supply of God's grace? Why do we so often seem to live in spiritual poverty instead of experiencing life to the full as Jesus promised (John 10:10)? There are several reasons that may or may not apply to a particular believer, but for the purposes of our study on grace, I'd like to look at two that probably apply to most of us.

First, is our frequent misperception of God as the divine equivalent of Ebenezer Scrooge; the God who demands the last ounce of work out of His people and then pays them poorly. That may sound like an overstatement of our perception of God, but I believe it is a fairly accurate representation of how many Christians think.

Perhaps the larger reason why we do not experience more of God's grace is our misconception that, having been saved by grace, we must now, at least to some degree, "pay our own way" and earn God's blessings in our daily lives. An accepted maxim among people today, "There is no such thing as a free lunch" (which may be true in our society), is carried by us into our relationship with God.

You and I actually experience the grace of God in our lives far more than we realize. But all too often we do not enjoy His grace because we are trying to live by merit, not by grace. In looking for our own goodness by which we hope to earn the blessing of God, we fail to see the superabundance of the goodness and grace of God in our lives. (Taken from chapters 3 and 4 of *Transforming Grace.*) 〞

EXPLORING GRACE

1. Read Romans 3:19-26. There are two aspects to our justification. First, God removes our guilt from us and places it upon Jesus. Second, He credits Jesus' righteousness to us. What practical difference does it make to your life that God has removed your sin and given you Jesus' righteousness? How should this fact affect the way you feel? The way you live?

2. It's easy to believe this doctrine of justification intel-
lectually, but many people find it hard to let this truth
strongly affect their lives. Why do you suppose that's
the case?

3. Read Ephesians 2:1-9. Fill in this chart to help show the
contrast Paul makes between what we deserve and what
God has done for us.

| Our spiritual condition before we have faith in Christ | What God has done for us in Christ |
| --- | --- |
| | |

4. What do the following verses show us about God's
forgiveness?

Psalm 103:12

Isaiah 38:17

22

Isaiah 43:25

Micah 7:19

5. Sometimes we know that God has forgiven us but we have trouble forgiving ourselves. Why do you think this is true?

**Barriers to Experiencing God's Forgiveness**

♦ A mistaken feeling that we must somehow suffer or pay for our own sins, at least to some degree. We often act like we think God's forgiveness only kicks in after we have reached some mysterious level of suffering for our own sins.

♦ A desire to hold on to our guilt so that we don't have to change our behavior. If I consider myself a terrible and guilty person then of course I will continue to sin. But if I know I am forgiven then I am truly free to go forward and improve, however slowly, in my behavior (Hebrews 9:14).

♦ Failure to cultivate our relationship with God. If we are not growing in our knowledge of who God is, through time in His Word and in conversation with Him, then we will also be out of touch with the forgiveness He is so ready to offer (Philippians 3:7-10).

23

6. Are there any areas of your life where you are not experiencing God's forgiveness? What factors in the list above may be part of why you are not experiencing God's forgiveness?

7. Believers fail to experience God's grace on a daily basis for many reasons. Two of these are:

   ◆ A misconception of God as a hard taskmaster who meets our needs begrudgingly.
   ◆ The belief that while we were saved by grace we must now "pay our own way" and earn God's blessings in our daily lives.

   It is possible to know that the above beliefs are lies and still operate as though they were true. Share a time when you were tempted to operate according to one of these misconceptions.

8. Decide to do one of the following things or else come up with your own plan to help you experience God's forgiveness more fully.

   a. Memorize one of the verses about God's forgiveness in question 4.

   b. Write a letter to the Lord confessing once and for all the things that you still feel He has not forgiven. Then burn the letter and thank Him that "He himself bore our sins in his body on the tree, so that we might die to sins and live for righteousness; by his wounds you have been healed" (1 Peter 2:24).

c. Ask a close friend to get together with you for a time of prayer. Turn your past sins over to the Lord, once and for all. When doubts come in, dispel them with the memory of that specific time when your sins were confessed and forgiven.

d. Write down the lie you are tempted to believe about God (see question 7). Tell God you know it's a lie and ask Him to do whatever He needs to do to teach your heart the truth about this.

## CLOSING PRAYER

Thank the Lord that He "does not treat us as our sins deserve or repay us according to our iniquities" (Psalm 103:10).

GOING DEEPER (Extra questions for further study)

1. What does it mean when we say that Christ made atonement for our sins? Look at the following verses and see how they help you understand atonement.

John 3:36

Romans 3:25


Hebrews 2:17


1 John 2:2, 4:10


2. Fill in the following chart based on Titus 3:3-7.

| Characteristics of man and what he has done | Characteristics of God and what He has done |
| --- | --- |
| | |

3. Is it possible to go beyond the point where God can forgive? Explain how a person might feel he has sinned one too many times to receive God's forgiveness, and why those feelings are wrong.

4. Read Colossians 1:21-22. Does the phrase "free from accusation" describe the way you think about yourself? Why, or why not?

5. What do the following verses say about how God wants to treat us?

Jeremiah 29:10-11

Jeremiah 32:38-41

PONDERING GRACE (For personal reflection)

*Guilty, vile and helpless we; Spotless Lamb of God was he; Full atonement! Can it be? Hallelujah! What a Savior!*

Philip P. Bin

*The generosity and the magnanimity of God are so great that he accepts nothing from us without rewarding it beyond all computation. . . . The vast disproportion existing between our work and God's reward of it displays his boundless grace, to say nothing of the gift of salvation which is made before we have even begun to do any work.*

R. C. H. Lenski,
*The Interpretation of St. Matthew's Gospel*

27

*Perhaps the most difficult task for us to perform is to rely on God's grace and God's grace alone for our salvation. It is difficult for our pride to rest on grace. Grace is for other people—for beggars. We don't want to live by a heavenly welfare system. We want to earn our own way and atone for our own sins. We like to think that we will go to heaven because we deserve to be there.*

R. C. Sproul

# DOES GOD HAVE A RIGHT?

## CENTRAL IDEA

**God does not owe us anything. All we have comes graciously from His hand, therefore we should be content and grateful for the lot in life He has given us. In Christ we are blessed with all spiritual riches, and in Christ all of God's promises are fulfilled.**

## WARM-UP

Imagine for a moment that you have worked hard for several years to save enough money to buy a car and that a close friend's parents simply hand him money for a new car.

◆ How do you feel toward your friend? How do you feel about your own circumstances?

◆ How do you think you should feel?

## DOES GOD HAVE A RIGHT?

❝ There is a very high sense of entitlement within modern society. Older people feel *entitled* to certain benefits from the government. Middle-aged people feel *entitled* to generous health and retirement benefits from their employers. Younger adults feel *entitled* to immediately enjoy the same standard of living their parents took years to achieve. And young people feel *entitled* to whatever material luxuries they desire.

Many observers of our culture are quite concerned about this pervasive sense of "rights" and expectations within our society as a whole. But for Christians, such a high sense of entitlement is especially detrimental to our spiritual lives. For one thing, God supplies all our needs and desires. Every good gift is from Him, regardless of the intermediate means through which that gift is supplied. As James said, "Every good and perfect gift is from above, coming down from the Father of the heavenly lights, who does not change like shifting shadows" (James 1:17). However, God, through His providential workings, almost always uses some person or institution or other human instrumentality to meet our needs. Ultimately, though, He is the One who provides or withholds what we desire or think we need.

Because of the influence of our culture, we begin to be as demanding of our "rights" before God as we are toward people. It is bad enough, and certainly not very Christian, to have the attitude "The world owes me something just because I am," but to have the attitude that *God* owes me something is exceeding dangerous to spiritual health. It will ruin our relationship with God, nullify our effectiveness in ministry, and perhaps turn us bitter or resentful. Unlike our government, or school, or family, or employer, God will not "give in" to our sense of rights or respond to pressure tactics. We never win the battle of "rights" with God. He cares too much about our spiritual growth to let that happen.

Where does an emphasis on the fact that God doesn't owe us anything leave us? In a word it leaves us *content*, and "godliness with contentment is great gain" (1 Timothy 6:6).

Contentment with what we have—whether it is possessions, or station in life, or mental or physical abilities—is worth far, far more than all the things we don't have.

I'm not suggesting we should always be satisfied with the status quo in every area of our lives and not pray for or seek improvement. Remember, God by His nature is graciously disposed to give us all good things (Romans 8:32). But for all of us, there are certain things that are simply not going to change. In those areas we must learn to be content, always accepting the fact that God does not owe us something different.

The apostle Paul wrote, "For no matter how many promises God has made, they are 'Yes' in Christ. And so through him the 'Amen' is spoken by us to the glory of God" (2 Corinthians 1:20). What did Paul mean when he said all God's promises are "Yes" in Christ?

First of all, Christ in His Messianic mission is the personal fulfillment of all the promises in the Old Testament regarding a Savior and coming King. Beyond the actual fulfillment of all the promises made about Him, Christ is also the meritorious basis upon which all of God's other promises depend.

As John Calvin wrote, "It is only in Christ that God the Father is graciously inclined toward us. His promises are the testimonies of His fatherly goodwill towards us."[1] Thus it follows that they are fulfilled only in Christ.

Think just now of what you feel your greatest needs are, both spiritually and temporally. As you bring those needs to God in prayer, which would you rather present to Him as a consideration for meeting those needs: your spiritual disciplines, your obedience, and your sacrifice, imperfect as they are; or the infinite and perfect merit of Jesus? To ask the question is to answer it, is it not?

I don't mean to disparage any spiritual discipline, commitment, or sacrifice. These all have their place in the realm of grace. But they are never to be relied on as a meritorious cause for expecting God's blessing or answer to prayer.

If only we will learn to rest our entire case on the merits of Jesus Christ, instead of our own, and to be content with what God gives instead of demanding rights, we will learn the joy of living by grace and not by works. (Taken from chapter 5 of *Transforming Grace*.) 99

## EXPLORING GRACE

1. Matthew 20:1-16 is the story of a generous landowner. Read this story and then answer these questions.

a. Assuming the landowner represents God, what do we learn about the character of God from this story?

b. What can you observe about human nature and how people tend to respond to the good fortune of others?

c. With which worker do you identify?

d. Why do people tend to think of the landowner as unfair instead of generous?

e. What does this story tell us about what God's grace means?

2. Luke 7:1-10 is another helpful story. Read this story and then answer the following questions.

a. On what basis did the Jewish elders appeal to Jesus to heal the centurion's servant? (See verses 4-5.)

b. What was the centurion's perspective on what he deserved? (See verses 6-7.)

c. Do you tend to operate like the elders or the centurion?
Explain.


3. a. According to Luke 17:10, what sort of attitude are we
to have about the things we do for the Lord?



b. How easy is it for you to feel that way?




4. We are told in 1 Timothy 6:6 that if we stop expecting or
demanding certain things, we will enjoy contentment.

a. Are you failing to experience contentment in some
areas of your life? If so, name some areas in which
you struggle.




b. In which of these areas do you need to take some
action?

c. In which areas do you need a change of attitude?

5. We are not created equal, nor are we given equal opportunities throughout life. Each of us has our own unique set of circumstances. Those of some people are much more favorable than others. How do you think God wants us to respond to this fact?

6. Read 2 Corinthians 1:20.

   a. What does this verse tell you about God's promises and how they are filled?

   b. How does this verse help you let go of your expectations and focus on what God has already done?

CLOSING PRAYER

Search your heart. Do you base your hope for improved circumstances in your life on trust in God's love and contentment with whatever He decides, or do you focus on what you think you deserve? Do you think your attitude expresses more humble trust or resentful demanding? On your own, take a few minutes to write out a prayer expressing your thoughts and feelings to the Lord. Those who want can pray their prayers as you pray for the needs shared during your discussion.

GOING DEEPER (Extra questions for further study)

1. What do the following verses say about our right to demand anything from God?

Job 41:11

Romans 11:35

2. Today in our society we tend to have high expectations and a strong sense of our rights. Give some examples of these attitudes.

3. What do the following verses tell us about the source of all that we have?

1 Chronicles 29:14,16

Isaiah 26:12

Acts 17:25

James 1:17

4. The world is set up on a system of rewards for achievement at school and in the work place. Why doesn't God use the same system when it comes to our relationship with Him?

PONDERING GRACE (For personal reflection)

*See the two groups of laborers as they wend their way home that evening. As to amount of money in their pockets, they are all equal; but as to amount of content in their spirits there is a great difference. The last go home each with a penny his pocket, and astonished gratitude in his heart; their reward accordingly is a penny, and* more. *The first, on the contrary, go home each with a penny in his pocket, and corroding discontent in his soul; their reward accordingly is* less *than a penny.*

William Arnot, *Parables of Our Lord*

*Blessings at times come to us through our labors and at times without out labors, but never because of our labors; for God always gives them because of His undeserved mercy.*

Martin Luther

*Grace is not sought nor bought nor wrought. It is a free gift of Almighty God to needy mankind.*

Billy Graham

---

NOTE

1. John Calvin, *Calvin's New Testament Commentaries*, vol. 10, *The Second Epistle of Paul the Apostle to the Corinthians and the Epistles to Timothy, Titus and Philemon*, David W. Torrance and Thomas F. Torrance, eds., T. A. Smail, trans. (Grand Rapids, MI: Wm. B. Eerdmans Publishing Co., 1964 edition), pages 21-22.

# COMPELLED BY LOVE

## CENTRAL IDEA

**When we understand God's magnificent and boundless grace, we become motivated by gratitude and love to respond with a life devoted to Him.**

## WARM-UP

Think about some of the people you come in contact with regularly (neighbors, workmates, family, friends, acquaintances). What appear to be the basic motives behind why they live the way they live and why they make the decisions they make? (There is no need to be overly personal or specific about exactly whose life you are drawing conclusions from.)

## COMPELLED BY LOVE

66 We are not only justified by grace through faith, we *stand* every day in this same grace. And just as the preaching of justification by grace is open to misunderstanding, so is the teaching of living by grace.

The solution to this problem is not to add legalism to grace. The solution is to be so gripped by the magnificence and boundless generosity of God's grace that we respond out of gratitude rather than out of a sense of duty.

We have loaded down the gospel of grace in Christ

with a lot of "oughts." "I ought to do this," and "I ought to do that." "I ought to be more committed, more disciplined, more obedient." When we think or teach this way, we are substituting duty and obligation for a loving response to God's grace.

I firmly believe in and seek to practice commitment, discipline, and obedience. I am thoroughly committed to submission to the lordship of Jesus Christ in every area of my life. And I believe in and seek to practice other commitments that flow out of that basic commitment. I am committed to my wife "until death do us part." I am committed to integrity and fairness in business relationships. I am committed to seek to act in love toward everyone. But I am committed in these areas out of a grateful response to the grace of God, not to try to earn God's blessings.

Even our Christian terminology betrays the way we dichotomize the Christian life into "grace" and "works" compartments. We speak of the *gift of salvation* and the *cost of discipleship*. The "cost of discipleship" is not necessarily an unbiblical expression, but the connotation we build into it is. We often convey the idea that God's grace barely gets us inside the door of the Kingdom, and after that, it's all our own blood, sweat, and tears.

Our *motivation* for commitment, discipline and obedience is as important to God, perhaps even more so, than our *performance*. God searches the heart and understands every motive. To be acceptable to Him, our motives must spring from a love for Him and a desire to glorify Him. Obedience to God performed from a legalistic motive—that is, a fear of the consequences or to gain favor with God—is not pleasing to God.

Living under the grace of God instead of under a sense of duty frees us from the self-serving motivation of trying to earn God's favor. It frees us to obey God and serve Him as a loving and thankful response to Him for our salvation and for blessings already guaranteed to us by His grace. Consequently, a heartfelt grasp of God's grace—far from creating an indifferent or careless attitude in us—will actually provide us the only motivation that is pleasing to Him. Only when we are thoroughly convinced that the Christian life is entirely of grace are we able to serve Him out of a grateful and loving heart.

When I stress a God-ward motivation for our discipline and obedience, I am not talking about inclination or feeling. We are not to wait until we "feel like" having a quiet time to have one. And we certainly are not to wait until we are so inclined to obey God's commands. Motive has nothing to do with feelings or inclination; rather, it refers to the *reason* why we do, or don't do, something. For the person living by grace, that reason should be a loving response to the abundant grace of God already manifested in Christ.

As we grow in grace, we will grow in our motivation to obey God out of a sense of gratitude and reverence to Him. Our obedience will always be imperfect in performance in this life. We will never perfectly obey Him until we are made perfect by Him. In the same way, our motives will never be consistently pure; there will frequently be some "merit points" mentality mixed in with our genuine love and reverence for God.

So don't be discouraged if you realize your motives have been largely merit-oriented. Just begin now to move toward grace motives. Begin to think daily about the implications of the grace of God in your life. Ask God to motivate you by His mercy and love. When you recognize merit-oriented motives at work in you, renounce them and cast yourself completely on the grace of God and the merit of Jesus Christ. As you grow in grace in this way, you will indeed discover that His love compels you to live, not for yourself, but for Him who died for you and was raised again. (Taken from chapter 6 of *Transforming Grace*.) **99**

## EXPLORING GRACE

1. a. Read 1 Chronicles 28:9, Proverbs 16:2, and 1 Corinthians 4:5. Why do you think our motives are so important to God?

b. Do you believe that the people you come in contact with think much about the motives behind their actions? Explain.

2. How does an understanding of God's grace help give us the right motives for the way we live?

3. a. How do our motives affect the outcome of what we do?

b. Give an example of how the wrong motives can completely undermine a good action.

4. a. Read the following verses and list some of the wrong motives people can have for trying to live a "good" life.

John 12:42-43

Galatians 6:12-13

Ephesians 2:8-9

Colossians 2:16-23

   b. What other wrong motives can drive people's actions?

5. a. Look at the following verses and list some of the pure or godly motives that *should* be behind our actions.

Romans 12:1

2 Corinthians 5:14-15

2 Corinthians 7:1

Colossians 3:12-14,23-24

Revelation 4:11

b. What other good motives can people have?

6. Do you think it is possible to keep your motives pure at all times? Explain.

7. Examine for a moment the motivations behind some of your actions. For each of the following areas of your life, determine how often you think you are motivated by impure motives instead of pure or godly motives. Rate your motives on a scale of 1 to 5 (1 = impure motives, 5 = godly motives). Do this individually. Then a few people can share their thoughts after doing this exercise.

___ Time spent in prayer

___ Time spent in praise and worship

___ Bible study

___ Bible reading

___ Memorizing Scripture

___ Building relationships with nonChristians

___ Helping young Christians grow

___ Fellowship with other believers

___ Serving others

___ Giving financially to God

8. In the previous question you may have become aware of some less-than-pure motives in your life. What do you think a person can do to help purify his or her motives in an area?

9. Take a minute to choose one of the following ways to work on having the right motives this week, or to come up with your own plan.

   a. Write in a journal every day for a week. Try to be especially aware of your motives during the day. When you recognize poor motives confess this to the Lord. Ask Him to help you sort out whether you need to change some of your actions, or change the way you think about these activities.

   b. Memorize one of the following verses. Remind yourself of the vastness of God's grace when you fall into doing things to try to earn His love.

      ◆ Jeremiah 31:3
      ◆ Romans 8:38-39 (For a bigger challenge memorize a larger portion or all of Romans 8.)
      ◆ Romans 12:1-2
      ◆ 2 Corinthians 5:14-15
      ◆ Ephesians 2:8-10

c. Spend an extra hour in prayer and meditation. Make a list of all the things you do on a weekly basis to serve God and to enhance your relationship with Him. Ask the Lord to help you evaluate your commitments and the motives behind them. Use the following questions to help you think through what He is doing in your life.

◆ Are there "good" things you are doing that you do primarily to please other people? Is it possible that God may want you to give up any of these?
◆ Have you failed to make commitments that you know the Lord has asked you to make?

## CLOSING PRAYER

Romans 12:1-2 gives us a beautiful picture of how we should respond to the grace of God. Read this passage and then write your thoughts in the form of a prayer. Let those who feel comfortable pray their prayers out loud.

GOING DEEPER (Extra questions for further study)

1. a. Share a time when you felt pressured by a sense of duty and obligation in your Christian life instead of a sense of joy, peace, and love.

   b. What was the source of this sense of drudgery in your life?

   c. What helped you put things back in the right perspective?

2. a. If a person does something even though he doesn't feel like doing it, does that mean his motives are wrong? Explain.

   b. How are our feelings and motivations related?

PONDERING GRACE (For personal reflection)

*The biggest gap in the world is the gap between the justice of a cause and the motives of the people pushing it.*

John P. Grier

*A lawdriver insists with threats and penalties; a preacher of grace lures and incites with divine goodness and compassion shown to us, for he wants no unwilling works and reluctant services; he wants joyful and delightful services of God.*

Martin Luther

*The Law's demands are inward, touching motive and desire, and are not concerned solely with outward action.*

Ernest F. Kevan,
*The Grace of Law*

*Our only business is to love God, and delight ourselves in Him. All kinds of disciplines, no matter how rugged, are quite useless if not motivated by love for God.*

Brother Lawrence,
*The Practice of the Presence of God*

# THE PROOF OF LOVE

## CENTRAL IDEA

**As followers of Jesus Christ we are set free to obey the moral laws of God out of love for Him. His ultimate purpose for us is that, through the enabling influence of the Holy Spirit, we will become more like Jesus.**

## WARM-UP

◆ What did you observe in your life this week as you thought more about the motives behind your actions?

◆ What difference has observing your motives made to your thoughts or your actions?

## THE PROOF OF LOVE

❝ One issue believers frequently struggle with is the relationship between living by grace and obedience to God's commands. Jesus clearly taught that our love for God will be expressed in obedience to Him. In fact, in the short space of nine verses, Jesus reiterates this thought three times: "If you love me, you will obey what I command. . . . Whoever has my commands and obeys them, he is the one who loves me. . . . If anyone loves me, he will obey my teaching" (John 14:15,21,23).

Our love for God, expressed through our obedience to

Him, is to be a response to His love, not a means of earning it. So one clear evidence that we are living by grace is a loving obedience to the commands of God. Anyone who thinks, *Since God's love is not conditioned on my obedience, I am free to live as I please,* is not living by grace, nor does he understand grace. What he perceives as grace is really a caricature of grace.

Jesus said that if we love Him, we will obey His commands. Now a command suggests two things. First, it gives clear direction. We are told what to do or not to do. We are not left in doubt as to how we are to live. The commands in the Bible provide a clear set of moral standards. The second aspect of a command is that it carries the idea of authority. A command implies that the one giving it has the authority to require obedience and the intention of doing it. This is true of the commands of God.

Some people believe that, under grace, God's law no longer has the meaning of requirement but is now an expression of His desire. They would readily say God *desires* that we be holy, but God does not *require* that we be holy. In other words, to assign the concept of requirement to the will of God is legalism, but to assign the concept of desire to it is grace.

I believe such a view is a misunderstanding of grace. God's grace does not change the fundamental character of God's moral law. Rather, the grace of God provides for the forgiveness and acceptance of those who have broken the law. The good news of the gospel is that God has removed the guilt we incur by breaking His law and has bestowed on us the righteousness of Christ, who perfectly kept His law. Legalism does not consist in yielding obedience to the law. Rather, it is to seek justification and good standing with God through the merit of works done in obedience to the law—instead of by faith in Christ.

So the fundamental character of God's law has not changed. What has changed is our *reason* for obedience, or our *motives*. Under a sense of legalism, obedience is done with a view to meriting salvation or God's blessing on our lives. Under grace, obedience is a loving response to salvation already provided in Christ.

50

The principle of love is not a "higher principle" over God's moral law. Rather, it provides the motive and the motivation for obedience, while the law provides the direction for the biblical expressions of love. The actions prescribed by God's law would be hollow indeed if they were not motivated by love for both God and our neighbor. I would much rather do business with someone who wanted to treat me fairly because he loved me than someone who deals fairly only because "it's good for business." I would also want his love to be guided by the moral and ethical principles of the Bible.

We have been set free from the bondage and curse that results from breaking the law. And we have been called to freedom from works as a means of trying to obtain any merit with God. But we have not been called to a freedom from the law as an expression of God's will for our daily living.

God's ultimate goal for us is that we might be truly conformed to the likeness of His Son. All through the New Testament we see this ultimate end in view as the writers speak of salvation.

There is an initial act of sanctification when God creates within us a new heart and gives us an entirely new disposition toward God and His will.

We must have a threefold view of sanctification or holiness. Our holiness is first of all an objective, perfect holiness, which is ours by virtue of our union with Christ who is perfectly holy. Then there is an initial act of sanctification in which a person's basic disposition toward God and His law is changed. This change is experienced by the believer but is not dependent upon the believer. It is solely a work of the Holy Spirit.

Finally this initial act of sanctification is followed up by the continuous action of the Holy Spirit throughout our lives as He works in us "to will and to act according to his good purpose" (Philippians 2:13). This progressive sanctification very much involves our activity. But it is an activity that must be carried out in dependence upon the Holy Spirit. It is not a partnership with the Spirit in the sense that we each—the believer and the Holy Spirit—do our respective tasks. Rather, we work as He enables us to work. His work lies behind all our work and makes our work possible.

In every one of these views of sanctification we see the grace of God. God in His grace sees us as perfectly holy in Christ. God in His grace sends His Holy Spirit to create a new heart within us and to write His law on our hearts, thus changing our basic disposition. And God in His grace continues to work in us through His Spirit to transform us more and more into the likeness of His Son. (Taken from chapters 7 and 8 of *Transforming Grace.*) **99**

## EXPLORING GRACE

1. Read John 14:15,21,23.

    a. Why do you think obedience is such an important way to express our love to God?

    b. What do you suppose often makes obedience so difficult?

    c. Share a time when you showed the Lord your love through an act of obedience.

2. a. Ephesians 5:17 tells us to "understand what the Lord's will is." God's will is revealed to us in the specific directions given in the ethical commands of Scripture. How does our attitude toward these commands change when we understand His grace and the purpose of the commands?

   b. What attitudes toward God's commands do the following writers express?

   Psalm 19:7-11

   Psalm 119:97

   Romans 7:12

   1 John 5:2-3

3. Galatians 5:6 gives a good summary of what God wants from us: "The only thing that counts is faith expressing itself through love." In what ways is your faith expressing itself through love at present in your particular circumstances?

4. a. What is the ultimate goal of our obedience?

   Romans 8:29

   2 Corinthians 3:18

   Philippians 1:9-11

   b. What difference does knowing this goal make to you?

5. Read Romans 13:8-10. Describe the relationship between the laws given to Moses and the two greatest commandments that Jesus states in Matthew 22:37-40.

6. The laws of Moses that deal with moral issues are still an important standard because they are the natural outcome of love. Explain what you believe the right decision

would be in each of the following situations. How do the Ten Commandments influence your decision, and how is this actually the decision of love?

a. A man meets a woman he finds very attractive. She has the potential to be a close friend in a way his wife has not been. What should he do and not do in relating to this woman? What should he do in his relationship with his wife?

b. A young woman finds that she is pregnant with her fourth child. Her husband has just informed her that he is having an affair and will file for divorce. She has no way to support herself. Should she consider having an abortion? Why, or why not?

c. A family is struggling to survive. They never have enough to eat and other necessities are scarce. The husband has an opportunity to make a lot of money on a business deal if he tells some lies in the process. What should he do?

7. Many excellent passages in the Bible spell out guidelines for living. The Holy Spirit uses these passages to show us what He wants to change in our lives. We are active participants in this process of sanctification. In dependence upon His help, we must respond in obedience. We must ask Him to change our inward disposition so that we want to obey and then we must ask Him for the power to obey.

Read all of Colossians 3 on your own. Ask God to show you what He wants to do in your life this week. Write down your thoughts. If you feel comfortable, share your thoughts with the group. Accountability to others is a great help when it comes to making difficult changes.

## CLOSING PRAYER

Reread Psalm 19:7-11 as a part of your prayer time. Express your gratitude to the Lord for His perfect commands. Ask Him for the grace to respond to His work in your life more fully this week.

### GOING DEEPER (Extra questions for further study)

1. Read 1 Thessalonians 4:3. Do you think that growing in our faith is optional?

2. Read Ephesians 4:22-24 and Philippians 2:12-13. Put into your own words the relationship between God's work in our lives and our own effort in the process of sanctification.

3. Although we could never earn our salvation or any blessings we now enjoy as Christians, God cares about how
we choose to live our lives. According to the following
verses, how does God feel about the things we do?

Ephesians 4:30

Ephesians 5:8-10

1 Timothy 2:1-3

1 Timothy 5:4

PONDERING GRACE (For personal reflection)

*Moral law is more than a test; it is for man's own good. Every
law that God has given has been for man's benefit. If man
breaks it, he is not only rebelling against God; he is hurting
himself.*

Billy Graham

*The beginning and the end of the law is kindness.*

Jewish proverb

*If Jesus gave us a command He could not enable us to fulfill,
He would be a liar; and if we make our inability a barrier
to obedience, it means we are telling God there is something
He has not taken into account. Every element of self-reliance*

57

*must be slain by the power of God. Complete weakness and dependence will always be the occasion for the Spirit of God to manifest His power.*

Oswald Chambers, *My Utmost for His Highest*

*The great mistake made by most of the Lord's people is in hoping to discover* in themselves *that which is to be found in Christ alone.*

Arthur W. Pink, *The Doctrine of Sanctification*

*Joy is love exalted; peace is love in repose; long-suffering is love enduring; gentleness is love in society; goodness is love in action; faith is love on the battlefield; meekness is love in school; and temperance is love in training.*

Dwight L. Moody

# CALLED TO BE FREE

## CENTRAL IDEA

**As followers of Christ we are free. Free from the drive to earn God's favor by our actions. Free from the oppression of trying to live up to manmade religious rules and regulations. Free to let the Holy Spirit create in our lives something beautiful and pleasing to God.**

## WARM-UP

What thoughts come to your mind when you hear the word *freedom*?

## CALLED TO BE FREE

**"**Legalism is, first of all, anything we do or don't do in order to *earn* favor with God. It is concerned with rewards to be gained or penalties to be avoided. This is a legalism we force on ourselves.

Second, legalism insists on conformity to manmade religious rules and requirements, which are often unspoken but are nevertheless very real. To use a more common expression, it requires conformity to the "do's" and "don'ts" of our particular Christian circle. We force this legalism on others or allow others to force it on us. It is conformity to how other people think we should live instead of how the Bible tells us to live. More often than not, these rules have no valid biblical basis.

Despite God's call to be free, we are often more afraid of indulging the sinful nature than we are of falling into legalism. Yet legalism does indulge the sinful nature because it fosters self-righteousness and religious pride. It also diverts us from the real issues of the Christian life by focusing on external and sometime trivial rules.

Manmade rules is a prevalent way in which legalism creeps into our lives. We build fences, or make rules, to keep ourselves from committing certain sins. Soon these fences—instead of the sins they were designed to guard against—become the issue. We elevate our rules to the level of God's commandments.

Many of our "do's and don'ts" begin as a sincere effort to deal with real sin issues by building a fence. But very often we begin to focus on the fence instead of the sin it was designed to guard against. We fight our battles in the wrong places; we deal with externals instead of the heart.

Should we scrap our fences, then? Not necessarily. Often they are helpful; sometimes they are necessary. But we have to work at keeping them in perspective—just fences, helpful to us but not necessarily applicable to others. We also have to work at guarding our freedom from other people's fences.

A second area of legalism arises from believers holding differing opinions about certain practices. God allows equally godly people to have differing opinions on certain matters. We tend to universalize God's particular leading in our lives and apply it to everyone else.

When we think like that we are, so to speak, "putting God in a box." We are insisting that He must surely lead everyone as we believe He has led us. We refuse to allow God the freedom to deal with each of us as individuals. When we think like that, we are legalists.

We must not seek to bind the consciences of other believers with our private convictions that arise out of our personal walk with God. Even if you believe God has led you in developing those convictions, you still must not elevate them to the level of spiritual principles for everyone else to follow. If we are going to enjoy the freedom we have in Christ, we must be alert to convictions that fall into the category of differing opinions. We must not seek to bind the consciences of others or allow them to bind ours. We must stand firm in the freedom we have in Christ.

Another area where we tend to become legalistic is about the activities I call spiritual disciplines: having regular private devotions, studying the Bible, memorizing Scripture, meeting with a group Bible study, or faithfully attending a weekly prayer meeting.

We should actively promote spiritual disciplines. They are absolutely necessary for growth in our Christian lives. And since ours is a largely undisciplined age, many believers are losing out on the benefits of those disciplines that could help them grow to maturity in Christ. But we should promote them as benefits, not as duties. Perhaps we should stop talking about being "faithful" to have a quiet time with God each day, as if we were doing something to earn a reward. It would be better to talk about the *privilege* of spending time with the God of the universe and the importance for our own sake of being consistent in that practice.

Another reason why we fail to enjoy our freedom in Christ is that we are afraid of what others will think. We do or don't do certain things because of a fear that we will be judged or gossiped about by others. But standing firm in our freedom in Christ means we have to resist the urge to live by the fear of what others think.

We've talked about fences, differing opinions, spiritual disciplines, and fear of what others think. These are only some of the areas in which we practice legalism with each other and with ourselves. We need to guard against these potential pitfalls and diligently apply ourselves to learning to live under the reign of God's transforming grace. (Taken from chapter 9 of *Transforming Grace*.) 99

### EXPLORING GRACE

1. a. Read 2 Corinthians 3:17 and Galatians 5:1,13. Why do you think God wants us to realize the freedom we have in Christ?

b. What does freedom do for the human spirit?

c. Why do you suppose man is so quick to relinquish his freedom and revert to living by manmade rules and regulations that foster conformity?

2. a. Galatians 5:16-18 helps us understand how our freedom in Christ leads not to license but rather to a life led by the Spirit. How do you sense the leading of the Spirit in your life?

b. Give an example of a time recently when you felt the Spirit leading you—in a difficult decision, in the way you responded to a particular situation, or in the way you responded to a particular person.

3. Many godly qualities will become dominant in our lives as we use our freedom to respond more and more to the Spirit. By God's grace, through the work of His Holy Spirit, these qualities are growing within us.

Below is a list of Christian character traits found in Galatians 5:22-23 and Colossians 3:12-15.

a. Share with the group the character traits you have seen in the lives of other members.

b. Which of these character traits do you think God is working to develop in your life?

| | |
|---|---|
| compassion | love |
| kindness | joy |
| humility | peace |
| gentleness | patience |
| forbearance | goodness |
| forgiveness | faithfulness |
| thankfulness | self-control |

4. Knowing that the Spirit brings these godly qualities into our lives, what do you think your role is in this process?

5. a. Legalism that requires adherence to manmade rules is unfortunately quite common in churches today. Can you think of some examples that you have observed?

b. What are some of the natural results or effects of this kind of legalism?

6. a. In Romans 14:1-23 Paul clearly states that God allows equally godly people to have differing opinions on certain matters. Read these verses and then think of a modern parallel to the issue of eating meat.

   b. How does Romans 14 help you better understand contemporary issues of differing opinions?

7. We tend to be legalistic with each other when it comes to spiritual disciplines (prayer, Bible study, Bible reading, witnessing, fasting, etc.). Due to our freedom in Christ, what do you believe should be our attitude toward these disciplines?

8. a. Sometimes we fail to enjoy the freedom we have in Christ because we are afraid of what others will think. Can you give an example of a time when you worried about what others would think when you were doing something you knew God had given you the freedom to do?

b. How did you handle the situation?

c. How would you handle it differently now?

## CLOSING PRAYER

Focus on thanking God for the freedom you enjoy as followers of Jesus Christ. Ask the Lord to help you respond more to the working of the Holy Spirit in your lives.

### GOING DEEPER (Extra questions for further study)

1. Did your parents establish rules or put up "fences" that you did not understand? Give an example.

2. If you have children, how have you explained the reasons for your boundaries to your children?

PONDERING GRACE (For personal reflection)

*A Christian man is the most free lord of all, and subject to none; a Christian man is the most dutiful servant of all, and subject to everyone.*

Martin Luther

*Only what God has commanded in his word should be regarded as binding; in all else there may be liberty of actions.*

John Owen

*Let us never surrender our judgments or our consciences to be at the disposal and opinions of others, and to be subjected to the sentences and determinations of men. . . . It is my exhortation therefore to all Christians to maintain their Christian freedom by constant watchfulness. You must not be tempted or threatened out of it; you must not be bribed or frightened from it; you must not let either force or fraud rob you of it.*

Samuel Bolton, *The True Bound of Christian Life*

# THE SUFFICIENCY OF GRACE

## CENTRAL IDEA

**God's grace enables us to persevere and grow despite any and all obstacles. God gives each of us the grace we need to fulfill the ministry and service He has given to us to bring glory to His Name.**

## WARM-UP

Give an example from the past week when God's grace was sufficient to enable you to meet some challenge.

## THE SUFFICIENCY OF GRACE

**"** Grace, as used in the New Testament, expresses two related and complimentary meanings. First, it is *God's unmerited favor to us through Christ whereby salvation and all other blessings are freely given to us.* Second, it is *God's divine assistance to us through the Holy Spirit.*

We have seen that God's grace assumes our sinfulness, guilt, and ill-deservedness. In the second meaning of grace, we see it also assumes our weakness and inability. Just as grace is opposed to the pride of self-righteousness, so it is also opposed to the pride of self-sufficiency.

God continually works to cause His people to realize their utter dependence on Him. We see that He does this through bringing each of us to the point of human extremity

67

where we have no place to turn but to Him.

God never allows pain without a purpose in the lives of His children. He never allows Satan, nor circumstances, nor any ill-intending person to afflict us unless He intends to use that affliction for our good. God never wastes pain. He always causes it to work together for our ultimate good, the good of conforming us more to the likeness of His Son (see Romans 8:28-29).

One of the more dramatic and prolonged illustrations of God teaching His people dependence on Him is found in His provision for the Israelite nation in the desert. God provided food for the Israelites through a continual miracle every day for forty years. God wanted the Israelites to realize and remember their utter dependence on Him, so He used an extremity of need and a miraculous provision to capture their attention and teach them a lesson that is difficult to learn. Still, they forgot. How much easier is it, then, for us to forget when God supplies our needs through ordinary, mundane ways.

It is even more difficult, however, for us to learn our dependence on God in the spiritual realm. A lack of money for food or to make the monthly mortgage payment gets our attention very quickly, and the need is obvious. The money is either available or it isn't. There's no pretending. But we can pretend in the spiritual realm. We can exist for months—going through the motions, perhaps even teaching Sunday school, or serving as an elder or deacon—depending on nothing more than mere natural human resources.

Before we can learn the sufficiency of God's grace, we must learn the *in*sufficiency of ourselves. The more we see our sinfulness, the more we appreciate grace in its basic meaning of God's undeserved favor. In a similar manner, the more we see our frailty, weakness, and dependence, the more we appreciate God's grace in its dimension of His divine assistance.

The Holy Spirit strengthens us and enables us to meet in a godly fashion *whatever circumstances* cross our paths. God's grace is not given to make us feel better, but to glorify Him. Modern society's subtle, underlying agenda is good feelings. We want the pain to go away. We want to feel better in difficult situations, but God wants us to glorify Him in those circumstances. Good feelings may come, or they may not, but that is not the issue. The issue is whether or not we honor God by the way we respond to our circumstances. God's grace—in the form of the enabling power of the Holy Spirit—is given to help us respond in such a way.

God's daily distribution of the manna to His people in the desert illustrates the way He distributes grace. There is always an ample supply; no one ever need go without. But there is only as much as we need—and even that is only on a day-to-day basis. God doesn't permit us to "store up" grace. We must look to Him anew each day for a new supply. Sometimes we must look for a new supply each hour!

In ourselves we are *weak, unworthy,* and *inadequate.* We really are! We are not denigrating ourselves when we recognize this truth. We are simply acknowledging reality and opening ourselves to the grace of God.

God's grace is sufficient for our weakness. Christ's worth does cover our unworthiness, and the Holy Spirit does make us effective in spite of our inadequacy. This is the glorious paradox of living by grace. When we discover we are weak in ourselves, we find we are strong in Christ. When we regard ourselves as less than the least of all God's people, we are given the immense privilege of serving in the Kingdom. When we almost despair over our inadequacy, we find the Holy Spirit giving us unusual ability. We shake our heads in amazement and say with Isaiah, "LORD, . . . all that we have accomplished you have done for us" (Isaiah 26:12).

This is the amazing story of God's grace. God saves us by His grace and transforms us more and more into the likeness of His Son by His Grace. In all our trials and afflictions, He sustains and strengthens us by His grace. He calls us by grace to perform our own unique function within the Body of Christ. Then, again by grace, He gives to each of us the spiritual gifts necessary to fulfill our calling. As we then serve Him, He makes that service acceptable to Himself by grace, and then rewards us a hundredfold by grace. (Taken from chapters 10 and 11 of *Transforming Grace.*) 〝

## EXPLORING GRACE

1. In 2 Corinthians 12:2-10 we find a powerful passage about suffering and the sufficiency of God's grace. Read this passage and then answer the following questions.

   a. What explanations does Paul give for why his physical suffering is not removed?

   b. Why do you suppose we don't always get a clear explanation of why we are allowed to suffer certain things?

   c. Why can God express His power in our lives better through our weaknesses than through our strengths?

2. Think of a weakness in your own life. It could be a physical problem, an emotional weakness, or difficult circumstances. In what specific ways have God's power and grace become real in your life through this trial?

3. About trials, James says that we are to "welcome them as friends" (James 1:2, PH). Read James 1:2-4.

    a. What do you think James means by welcoming trials as friends?

    b. Why does he encourage us to have this kind of attitude?

4. a. Do you tend to feel closer to God when your life is relatively trouble-free or when you have problems? Why do you think this is the case?

    b. Is it necessary for us to experience troubles to be close to God? Why, or why not?

c. What can a person who has a pretty easy life do to get close to God, short of praying for trials?

5. In the story of the Israelites' wanderings in the wilderness we see the total dependence of man upon God in a dramatic way. Read Deuteronomy 8:2-3.

a. Why do you think it seems so easy for us today to fall into the sin of thinking we are self-sufficient?

b. Why is it a sin to think we are self-sufficient?

c. Whether we realize it or not, we depend on God for far more than our physical needs. Is it easier for you to fall into an attitude of self-sufficiency in physical things or in spiritual things? Why do you suppose that's so?

6. In Romans 12:4-8, Paul explains that we each have different spiritual gifts. The Lord gives us these for the purpose

of fulfilling the ministry or service He has given us. Look also at the list of spiritual gifts in 1 Corinthians 12:4-11.

a. What spiritual gifts do you see evidence of in the lives of other group members?

b. It is often easier to see the spiritual gifts of others than to see our own gifts. Nonetheless, we should be aware of the gifts God has given us so that we can put ourselves in positions where those gifts can be used. What spiritual gift(s) do you think God has given to you?

c. Share a time when you were aware of God using your spiritual gift(s) in a specific situation.

7. Read 1 Corinthians 15:9-10 and Ephesians 3:8.

a. What was Paul's perspective on his own ability to fulfill the job God had given him to do?

b. What service or ministry has God given to you? (This could include raising your family, teaching Sunday school, being available for a friend in need, sharing the gospel with a neighbor, etc. If you have trouble answering this question, spend some time in prayer, asking God to show you ways you can begin to serve Him right where He has placed you.)

c. How do Paul's words help encourage you in whatever God is asking you to do?

8. Look at the following verses. How do they drive home the point that it is God who enables us in everything we do?

Isaiah 26:12

1 Corinthians 3:6

2 Corinthians 3:4-6

Colossians 1:28-29

9. As believers we will stand before the Lord and receive rewards by God's grace based upon how we have lived this life. All of our growth and strength for service come from God. All the fruit of our labors is the result of God's grace. We must labor. God doesn't do that for us. But we must labor in dependence on His grace to enable us. Read 1 Corinthians 3:7-15, 2 Corinthians 5:10, and Ephesians 6:7.

a. What is the basis of the rewards we receive as Christians?

b. What happens to the Christian whose labors have had no eternal value?

c. What is the purpose of these rewards? See Revelation 4:9-11.

10. a. In what area of your life do you sense the greatest need to experience of God's grace?

b. What barriers do you think you might be using to prevent God from working in your life?

## CLOSING PRAYER

Read aloud the poem by Annie Johnson Flint found in the "Pondering Grace" section. Then express your needs to the Lord and acknowledge His sufficiency. Confess your need to respond more to His working in your lives.

### GOING DEEPER (Extra questions for further study)

1. Read Philippians 4:4-13.

a. What is the secret to being content that Paul refers to in verse 12?

b. Have you learned to live by this secret in your own life? What specific things can you do to go deeper in living according to the principles Paul spells out in this passage?

2. What attitudes do the men in these passages display toward God in the midst of their suffering?

   Psalm 13

   Psalm 73:1-3,13-17,23-28

   Lamentations 3:19-33

3. What do the following verses say about how God works in our trials?

   Genesis 50:20

Romans 8:28-29

PONDERING GRACE (For personal reflection)

*The wilderness tested and disciplined the people in various
ways. On the one hand, the desolation of the wilderness
removed the natural props and supports which man by nature
depends on; it cast the people back on God, who alone could
provide the strength to survive the wilderness. On the other
hand, the severity of the wilderness period undermined the
shallow bases of confidence of those who were not truly
rooted and grounded in God. The wilderness makes or
breaks a man; it provides strength of will and character. The
strength provided by the wilderness, however, was not the
strength of self-sufficiency, but the strength that comes from a
knowledge of the living God.*

P. C. Craigie,
*The New International Commentary on the Old Testament,
The Book of Deuteronomy*

*For men have no taste for [God's power] till they are con-
vinced of their need of it and they immediately forget its value
unless they are continually reminded by awareness of their
own weakness.*

John Calvin, *Calvin's New Testament Commentaries*

*Day by day and with each passing moment,
Strength I find to meet my trials here;
Trusting in my Father's wise bestowment,
I've no cause for worry or for fear.
He whose heart is kind beyond all measure
Gives unto each day what He deems best—
Lovingly, its part of pain and pleasure,
Mingling toil with peace and rest.*

Lina Sandell Berg

78

*So [God] supplies perfectly measured grace to meet the needs of the godly. For daily needs there is daily grace; for sudden needs, sudden grace; for overwhelming need, overwhelming grace. God's grace is given wonderfully, but not wastefully; freely but not foolishly; bountifully but not blindly.*

John Blanchard,
*Truth for Life: A Devotional Commentary on the Epistle of James*

*He giveth more grace when the burdens grow greater;*
*He sendeth more grace when the labours increase;*
*To added afflictions he addeth his mercy,*
*To multiplied trials his multiplied peace.*

*When we have exhausted our store of endurance,*
*When our strength has failed ere the day is half done;*
*When we reach the end of our hoarded resources,*
*Our Father's full giving is only begun.*

*His love has no limits, his grace has no measure,*
*His power has no boundary known unto men;*
*For out of his infinite riches in Jesus,*
*He giveth, and giveth, and giveth again.*

Annie Johnson Flint

# APPROPRIATING GOD'S GRACE

## CENTRAL IDEA

**God's grace is applied to our lives and made real in our experience through prayer, the Bible, submission to His sovereignty, and the ministry of other believers.**

## WARM-UP

Describe a recent time when you experienced God's grace in a specific way. What did God use to give you this sense of His grace?

## APPROPRIATING GOD'S GRACE

**"** Perhaps the idea of *appropriating* the grace of God is a new thought to you, and you're not quite sure what I mean. The basic meaning of the word is "to take possession of," and that is what we do when we appropriate God's grace. We take possession of the divine strength He has made available to us in Christ. Now there are times when the Holy Spirit works in a sovereign way in our lives, apart from any appropriating activity on our part, but more often He expects us to act to appropriate His grace. To this end, He has provided four principal means of doing so: prayer, His word, submission to His providential workings in our lives, and the ministry of others.

The first avenue of appropriating God's grace is simply to ask for it in prayer. When we come to God's throne, we need to remember that He is indeed the God of all grace. He is the landowner who graciously gave a full day's pay to the workers who had worked only one hour in the vineyard. He is the God who said of the sinful nation of Israel even while they were in captivity, "I will rejoice in doing them good" (Jeremiah 32:41). He is the God who remained faithful to Peter through all his failures and sins and made him into a mighty apostle. He is the God who, over and over again, has promised never to leave us, nor forsake us (i.e., Deuteronomy 31:6,8; Psalm 94:14; Isaiah 42:16; Hebrews 13:5). He is the God who "longs to be gracious to you" (Isaiah 30:18), and He is the God who is for you, not against you (Romans 8:31). All this, and more, is summed up in that one statement, the God of *all* grace.

I believe all of us need to grasp more fully what it means to come to the throne of grace. We need to grasp in the depth of our souls what it means that we *do* have a High Priest, Jesus, who is able and disposed to sympathize with our weaknesses. Above all, we simply need to *go* to the throne of grace to find the grace to help in time of need.

Second, if we are to appropriate the grace of God, we must become intimate friends with the Bible. We must seek to know and understand the great truths of Scripture: truths about God and His character, and truths about man and his desperate need of God's grace.

The Bible is more than merely objective truth; it is actually life-giving and life-sustaining. Growth in the grace of God—whether that be His divine favor to the unworthy, or His divine enabling to the needy—requires growth in our assimilation of the Word of God. In the biological realm, assimilation is the process by which nourishment is changed into living tissue. In the spiritual realm, it is the process by which the written word of God is absorbed into our hearts and becomes, figuratively speaking, living spiritual tissue.

If we are to appropriate the grace of God, then, we must regularly expose ourselves directly to the word of God. It is not enough to only hear it preached or taught in our churches on Sundays, as important as those avenues are. We need a regular plan of reading, study, and yes, even memorization. Bible study and Scripture memorization earn no merit with God. We never earn God's blessing by doing these things any more than we earn His blessing by eating nutritious food. But as the eating of proper food is necessary to sustain a healthy physical life, so the regular intake of God's word is necessary to sustain a healthy spiritual life and to regularly appropriate His grace.

The third means God uses to administer His grace to us is our submission to His providential working in our lives. If we are to appropriate God's grace, we must humble ourselves, we must submit to His providential working in our lives. To do this we must first see His mighty hand behind all the immediate causes of our adversities and heartaches. We must believe the biblical teaching that God is in sovereign control of all our circumstances, and whatever or whoever is the immediate cause of our circumstances, God is behind them all.

The fourth principal means by which God ministers His grace to us is through the ministry of other believers. The times when we need an extra measure of God's grace are often the times when we are most reluctant to let other people know we need it. This leads to an important principle regarding the ministry of grace. Each of us needs to cultivate a small group of friends with whom we can be transparent and vulnerable. This might be on an individual or small group basis. But we need a few people—including our spouse, if we have one—with whom we feel free to share our failures, hurts, and sorrows.

There are three basic ways we can be ministers of God's grace to others: prayer, the word of God, and help in submitting to God's providence. Having experienced God's grace, we are then called on to extend that grace to others. The evidence of whether we are living by grace is to be found in the way we treat other people. If we see ourselves as sinners and totally unworthy in ourselves of God's compassion, patience, and forgiveness, then we will want to be gracious to others.

God's grace is indeed meant to be a transforming grace. I invite you and urge you to lay aside any remnant of self-goodness you may think you still have. Admit your total spiritual bankruptcy, and drink deeply from the infinite grace of God. And then in deep awareness of what you have received, extend that same spirit of grace to others. (Taken from chapters 12 and 13 of *Transforming Grace*.) 99

## EXPLORING GRACE

### Experiencing God's Grace Through Prayer

1. a. Hebrews 4:14-15 encourages us to go to God in prayer, asking for the grace we need. What does this passage give as some of the reasons why we can approach God with confidence? (See also Hebrews 2:18.)

   b. In what ways do you find any of those reasons encouraging?

2. If we are to experience God's grace through prayer, we must pray. But even for Christians this often seems to be the last thing we get around to doing.

   a. Why do you think many Christians don't pray more?

b. How do you feel about your prayer times at this point in your spiritual pilgrimage?

c. What specific things do you think you need to do to improve your prayer life?

## God's Grace Applied to Our Lives Through His Word

1. If we are to experience the grace of God, we must regularly expose ourselves to the word of God. God can bring His word to our attention in many ways, including:

   ◆ Friends
   ◆ Sermons
   ◆ Bible study
   ◆ Bible reading
   ◆ Christian books
   ◆ Bible memorization
   ◆ Christian radio and television

   a. Which of these are a part of a regular week for you?

b. Is there one area you believe you need to give more time to in your life? If so, which one?

2. a. Share a time when God used a particular Scripture passage in your life to speak directly to you.

b. By what means did you become aware of this passage at the time you needed it?

c. How did it help you in your particular situation?

**Receiving God's Grace**
**Through Humble Submission to Him**
1. To experience God's grace, we must humble ourselves and trust that God is in control regardless of the difficulty of our circumstances. Read 1 Peter 5:5-7.

a. What are we told to do in these verses?

b. What is the end result of our humility? When will we receive this end result?

c. In what areas of your life is God teaching you to be more humble?

2. a. Describe the attitude of a person who refuses to submit to what God is allowing into his life.

b. How is the grace of God restricted in this person's life?

c. Have you ever experienced a time when your attitude created a barrier in your life to enjoying the grace of God? Share what you learned from this experience.

**God's Grace Given to Us Through the Ministry of Others**

1. There are three basic ways that we can help one another respond to the Holy Spirit in our lives and thus receive God's grace.

    ◆ Pray for and with each other.
    ◆ Share relevant verses with each other.
    ◆ Help each other submit to the providence of God in our lives.

    a. We must have close relationships with other people if we want God to use those people in these three ways in our lives. How do you cultivate close relationships in your life?

    b. Give an example of a time when someone used one of these three ways to minister God's grace to you.

2. In order for God to use you to minister His grace to someone, that person must be receptive and open to your input. In the same way, we must communicate to others our willingness to let them minister to us.

    a. How good are you at letting others minister to you? Are you able to admit your needs to others?

b. How good are you at reading the signals from others as to when you could be a minister of God's grace in their lives?

## Appropriating God's Grace

1. a. Of the four ways that God can make His grace real in our lives discussed in this lesson, which one do you think you have the biggest problem with?

b. Take a few minutes to come up with a specific plan for how you will make yourself more available to God in that area this week.

## CLOSING PRAYER

Pray the following prayer as a group. Read one sentence at a time. Allow enough time of silence between sentences for each person to talk to God about specifics in his or her life that relate to this prayer.

Lord, I am willing to receive what You give.
Lord, I am willing to lack what You withhold.
Lord, I am willing to relinquish what You take.
Lord, I am willing to suffer what You inflict.
Lord, I am willing to be what You require.

GOING DEEPER (Extra questions for further study)

1. Colossians 3:12-14 gives us a list of qualities that are the result of God's grace at work in our lives.

    a. What do these verses say about how God thinks of us?

    b. How do the qualities listed in these verses enable us to be ministers of God's grace to others?

    c. Choose one of the qualities listed and commit to asking God every day for a week to increase that quality in your life.

2. Read Hebrews 7:25 and 1 John 2:1. How could the fact that Christ is interceding for you affect the way you pray?

3. a. What do the following verses teach us about God's sovereignty and the attitude we should have toward trials?

   Genesis 50:20

   Job 1:20-21

   Job 2:9-10

   b. How does trusting God and seeing His hand ultimately ruling in the circumstances of our lives help us maintain an attitude of humility?

4. Ecclesiastes 4:9-12 gives us a poetic description of how much we need one another. What are some of the reasons why we need strong friendships within the fellowship of believers?

PONDERING GRACE (For personal reflection)

*To pray is nothing more involved than to let Jesus come into our hearts, to give Him access with all His power to our needs. From this it is clear that success in prayer does not depend upon the assurance of the one who prays, nor upon his boldness, nor any such thing, but upon this one thing that he opens his heart to Jesus.*

O. Hallesby, *Prayer*

*Prayer is the exercise of drawing on the grace of God. Don't say—I will endure this until I can get away and pray. Pray* now; *draw on the grace of God in the moment of need.*

Oswald Chambers,
*My Utmost for His Highest*

*If the majesty and grace and power of God are not being manifested in us (not in our consciousness), God holds us responsible. "God is able to make all grace abound." Be stamped with God's nature, and His blessings will come through you all the time.*

Oswald Chambers,
*My Utmost for His Highest*

*God and the Word of his grace always go together; God lets his grace flow out through that Word.*

R. C. H. Lenski,
*The Interpretation of The Acts of the Apostles*

## Prayer Answered by Crosses

I asked the Lord that I might grow
    In faith and love and every grace,
Might more of his salvation know,
    And seek more earnestly his face.

'Twas he who taught me thus to pray;
    And he, I trust, has answered prayer;
But it has been in such a way
    As almost drove me to despair.

I hoped that, in some favoured hour,
    At once he'd answer my request
And by his love's constraining power
    Subdue my sins, and give me rest.

Instead of this, he made me feel
    The hidden evils of my heart,
And let the angry powers of hell
    Assault my soul in every part.

Yea, more with his own hand he seemed
    Intent to aggravate my woe,
Crossed all the fair designs I schemed,
    Blasted my gourds, and laid me low.

Lord, why is this? I trembling cried;
    Wilt thou pursue this worm to death?
This is the way, the Lord replied
    I answer prayer for grace and faith.

These inward trials I now employ
    From self and pride to set thee free,
And break thy schemes of earthly joy,
    That thou may'st seek thy all in me.

John Newton

# HELP FOR LEADERS

The following pages are designed to help a discussion leader guide a group in an edifying time centered on God's truth. You can appoint one person to lead each session, or you can rotate leadership.

## PREPARATION

Your aim as a leader is to create an environment that is conducive to study. You want the group members to feel comfortable with one another and to find the setting congenial. You want the session to be free from distractions.

*Personal Preparation.* As the group leader, your most important preparation for each session is prayer. You will want to make your prayers personal, of course, but here are some suggestions:

- ◆ Pray that group members will be able to attend the discussion. Ask God to enable them to feel free to share their thoughts and feelings honestly, and to contribute their unique gifts and insights.
- ◆ Pray for group members' private times with God this week. Ask God to be active in nurturing them.
- ◆ Ask God to give each of you new understanding and practical applications from the Scriptures as you talk. Pray that God will meet each person's unique needs.
- ◆ Ask for the Holy Spirit's guidance in exercising patience, acceptance, sensitivity, and wisdom. Pray

for an atmosphere of genuine love in the group, with each member being honestly open to learning and change.

♦ Pray that your discussion will lead each of you to obey the Lord more closely and demonstrate His presence.

♦ Pray for insight as you go over the study materials and for wisdom as you lead the group.

After prayer, your most important preparation is to be thoroughly familiar with the material you will discuss with the group. Make sure you have answered all of the questions. You will also find it important to read the chapters in *Transforming Grace* that are covered by each lesson. Decide which questions you want to discuss as a group. You may not have time to cover all the questions. Think about which questions are most important for your particular group to discuss. Questions in the *Going Deeper* section can be used in place of some of the questions in the *Exploring Grace* section. When a question is about a Scripture passage, it will be helpful to read the passage together. When there are a number of passages, you may want to choose ahead of time which ones to discuss.

*Group Preparation.* Choose a time and place to meet that is consistent, comfortable, and relatively free from distractions. Make plans to deal with children, pets, and ringing telephones. Refreshments can help people mingle, but don't let them consume too much of your time.

## THE FIRST SESSION

You may want to begin with a potluck supper. In this way, group members can get to know one another in the context of a meal, which is a good way to break down barriers. Then after dinner you can have your first session.

In this session, be sure to set aside adequate time for people to share who they are. It is amazing how much more productive and honest a Bible discussion is if the participants know each other.

At some point in the evening (probably toward the end),

go over the following guidelines. They help make a discussion more fruitful, especially when you are dealing with issues that truly matter to people.

*Confidentiality.* No one should repeat what someone shares in the group unless that person gives express permission. Even then, discretion is imperative. Be trustworthy. Participants should talk about their own feelings and experiences, not those of others.

*Attendance.* Each session builds on the previous ones, and you need each other. So, ask group members to commit to attending all eight sessions, unless an emergency arises.

*Participation.* This is a *group* discussion, not a lecture. It is important that each person participate in some way in the group.

*Preparation.* Decide as a group whether everyone will read the material and answer the questions before the group meets. Your discussions will be more interesting if group members have prepared in advance. In addition, group members will get far more out of the study if they have spent time thinking about the questions and meditating on the Scriptures before meeting. If group members are prepared it will not be necessary to take group time to read the excerpt or to look up *all* the Scripture references together.

*Honesty.* Appropriate openness is a key to a good group. Be who you really are, not who you think you ought to be.


## LEADING THE GROUP

Each session is designed to take sixty minutes:

- ◆ Ten minutes for opening prayer and warm-up questions;
- ◆ Forty minutes for discussion of the study questions;
- ◆ Ten minutes for closing prayer time.

***Work Toward a Relaxed and Open Atmosphere.*** This may not come quickly, so be a model for the others of acceptance, openness to truth and change, and love. Develop a genuine interest in each person's remarks, and expect to learn from them. Show that you care by listening carefully. Be affirming. Sometimes a hug is the best response.

*Pay Attention to How You Ask the Questions.* Don't ask, "What did you get for number 1?" Instead, by your tone of voice convey:

- ◆ your interest and enthusiasm for the question,
- ◆ your warmth toward the group.

The group will adopt your attitude. Read the questions as though you were asking them to good friends.

If the discussion falters:

- ◆ Be comfortable with silence. Let the group wrestle to think of answers. Don't be quick to jump in and rescue the group with your answers.
- ◆ Reword a question if the group members have trouble understanding it.
- ◆ If a question evokes little response, feel free to leave it and move on.
- ◆ Feel free to answer questions yourself occasionally. In particular, you should be the first one to answer questions about personal experiences. In this way you will model the depth of openness and thought you hope others will show. You can also model an appropriate length of response. Don't answer every question, but don't be a silent observer.
- ◆ If the discussion is winding down on a question, go on to the next one. It's not necessary to push people to see every possible angle.

*Ask Only One Question at a Time.* Often, participants' responses will suggest a follow-up question to you. Be discerning as to when you are following a fruitful train of thought and when you are going off on a tangent.

*Be Aware of Time.* Don't spend so much time discussing that you run out of time for application and prayer. Your goal is not to have something to discuss, but to become more like Jesus Christ.

*Encourage Constructive Controversy.* The group can learn a lot from struggling with the many sides of an issue. If you aren't threatened when someone disagrees, the whole group will be more open and vulnerable. Intervene, if necessary, to be sure that people are debating ideas and interpretations of Scripture, not attacking each other's feelings and character. If the group gets stuck in an irresolvable argument, say something like, "We can agree to disagree here," and move on.

*Don't Be the Expert.* People will stop talking if they think that you are judging their answers or that you think you know best. Let the Bible be the expert, the final say. Let people candidly express their feelings and experiences.

*Don't Do for the Group What It Can Do for Itself.* With a beginning group, you may have to ask all of the questions, do all of the outside research, plan the applications, etc. But within a few meetings you should start delegating various leadership responsibilities. Let members learn to exercise their gifts. Let them start making decisions and solving problems together. Encourage them to maturity and unity in Christ.

*Encourage People to Share Feelings as Well as Facts.* There are two dimensions of truth: the truth about how people feel, and the truth about who God is and what is right. People need to face both their real feelings and the real God.

*Summarize the Discussion Frequently.* Help the group see where the discussion is going.

*Let the Group Plan Applications.* The group and individual action responses in this guide are suggestions. Your group should adapt them so that they are relevant and life-changing for members. If group members aren't committed to an application, they won't do it. Encourage, but don't force.

*End with Refreshments.* Have coffee or soft drinks plus some cookies or cake, so that people will have an excuse to stay behind for a few extra minutes and discuss the subject informally. Often the most life-changing conversations occur after the formal session.


## AFTER THE DISCUSSION

Use these self-evaluation questions each week to help you improve your leadership next time:

1. Did you have the right number of questions prepared? Should you add to the next session's questions, or delete some?
2. Did you discuss the major issues?
3. Did you know your material thoroughly enough to have freedom in leading?
4. Did you keep the discussion from wandering?
5. Did everyone participate? Were people open?
6. Was anyone overtalkative? Undertalkative? Disruptive? Think about how you can handle these problems next week if they occur again.
7. Was the discussion practical? Did it lead to new understanding, new hope, repentance, change?
8. Did you begin and end on time?
9. Did you give the group the maximum responsibility that it can handle?

# OTHER GREAT BOOKS BY JERRY BRIDGES

## The Pursuit of Holiness

Holiness should mark the life of every Christian,
but holiness is often hard to understand. Learn what holiness is
and how to say no to the things that hinder it.

*The Pursuit of Holiness/$8*
Bible Study/$5

## The Practice of Godliness

It's easy to get caught up in doing things for God,
rather than being with God. Learn how to be godly in the midst
of daily life by being committed to God rather than activities.

*The Practice of Godliness/$10*
Bible Study/$5

## Trusting God

It's easy to trust God when everything is going your way.
But what about when things go wrong? This book will show you
essential truths about God we must believe to trust Him completely.

*Trusting God/$12*
Discussion Guide/$7

## The Discipline of Grace

If you've struggled with your role and God's role
in your growth as a Christian, this book will challenge you.
Learn to rest in Christ while pursuing a life of holiness.

*The Discipline of Grace/$12*
Discussion Guide/$6

Get your copies today at your local bookstore, or call
(800) 366-7788 and ask for offer **#2049**.

NAVPRESS

BRINGING TRUTH TO LIFE
www.navpress.org

# BIBLE STUDIES AND SMALL-GROUP MATERIALS FROM NAVPRESS

**BIBLE STUDY SERIES**
Design for Discipleship
Foundation for Christian Living
God in You
Learning to Love
The Life and Ministry of
    Jesus Christ
LifeChange
Love One Another
Pilgrimage Guides
Radical Relationships
Studies in Christian Living
Thinking Through Discipleship

**TOPICAL BIBLE STUDIES**
Becoming a Woman of Excellence
Becoming a Woman of Freedom
Becoming a Woman of Prayer
Becoming a Woman of Purpose
The Blessing Study Guide
Celebrating Life!
Growing in Christ
Growing Strong in God's Family
Homemaking
Husbands and Wives
Intimacy with God
Jesus Cares for Women
Jesus Changes Women
Lessons on Assurance
Lessons on Christian Living
Loving Your Husband
Loving Your Wife
A Mother's Legacy
Parents and Children
Praying from God's Heart
Strategies for a Successful
    Marriage
Surviving Life in the Fast Lane
To Run and Not Grow Tired
To Stand and Not Be Moved
To Walk and Not Grow Weary

What God Does When Men Pray
When the Squeeze is On

**BIBLE STUDIES WITH
COMPANION BOOKS**
Bold Love
Daughters of Eve
The Discipline of Grace
The Feminine Journey
From Bondage to Bonding
Hiding from Love
Inside Out
The Masculine Journey
The Practice of Godliness
The Pursuit of Holiness
Secret Longings of the Heart
Spiritual Disciplines for the
    Christian Life
Tame Your Fears
Transforming Grace
Trusting God
What Makes a Man?

**SMALL-GROUP RESOURCES**
201 Great Questions
Discipleship Journal's 101 Best
    Small-Group Ideas
How to Build a Small-Groups
    Ministry
How to Have Great Small-Group
    Meetings
How to Lead Small Groups
The Navigator Bible Studies
    Handbook
New Testament LessonMaker
The Small-Group Leaders
    Training Course

## NAVPRESS ◑
BRINGING TRUTH TO LIFE
www.navpress.org

Get your copies today at your local Christian bookstore, or call
(800) 366-7788 and ask for offer **NPBS**.